YOU'RE NUMBER ONE, NOW BELIEVE IT!

How to love, care and respect yourself in the midst of a setback

Naudia Lorraine

DOWNLOAD YOUR FREE WORKBOOK

THANK YOU!

As a small token of appreciation for choosing
to read my book, I would like to give you the FREE
workbook to enhance your ongoing
personal development journey.

Visit www.naudialorraine.com/ynonbworkbook for
your free workbook.

Contents

Introduction

As long as I can remember, my dad has always told my brother, sister, and me that we are number one. He instilled confidence in all three of us, and both my parents filled our lives with unconditional love and support.

But all the love and self-confidence in the world can't prevent setbacks from happening in your life. That's why, even during the hard times, it's important to love, respect, and care for yourself unconditionally. *You're Number One, Now Believe It!* is my story of overcoming setbacks and how they inspired my life's journey. It is geared to help fire up your self-love engines and put you back on a track filled with self-worth. YNONB will help you view yourself as a priority in your life without feelings of guilt.

It's so funny how certain things I did yesterday are completely forgotten but I can remember my first setback from over thirty years ago, as though it happened yesterday. In an attempt to reconnect with their homeland, my parents, after twenty years of living in England, decided to return 'home' to Jamaica. I was devastated. Here I was, nine years old, leaving my friends and extended family for a new country thousands of miles away from my 'home'.

I remember sitting in the waiting room at Heathrow Airport, with my life-like doll, Naomi, cradled in my arms. As I waited for our flight to leave, I stared off into the distance, watching planes land and leave through the humongous windows. The cavernous room, so cold and dark, felt like an appropriate tomb for my emotions.

My mom and sister who sat close by were oblivious to the sadness that overwhelmed me as I'm sure they were dealing with their own feelings of melancholy. Sitting there waiting for our flight to Montego Bay, I decided to make a vow to myself; a vow to never love anyone again so that I wouldn't have to feel the pain and hurt that was searing through my veins.

My first setback and I was already handling it wrong. I couldn't embrace the change; I only felt doom and gloom. The promise that I made to myself that day ended up lasting for over twenty years. A promise made to ease my pain ended up being a catalyst for my divorce all those years later... Lesson? Be careful what you wish for!

I am who I am because of what I've been through and because I have an innate need to survive in the midst of any storm. I've come back from setbacks because I love myself and I am number one to myself—with no feelings of selfishness. And yes, I am who I am because of what my parents instilled in me from a young age.

But it's never too late to learn, regardless of your background - or in my case, relearn how to love, respect, and care for yourself. You are more than worth it and deserve the best version of you.

Situations in life can knock the wind right out of your sails, but as we know, in survival of the fittest, only the strong will survive.

Every day is a new chance to invest in yourself wholeheartedly. If you've ever been through a setback that left you feeling broken, sad, and alone, then YNONB will show you how to love and care—not berate or harm—yourself.

During my divorce, I was so broken that I became a shell of myself. When I look back at that time, I don't even know who I was. Things that were out of character for me—such as unabashed flirting—became the norm. In retrospect, I clearly sought attention and validation that I was still desirable.

Finally, a solo trip to Belgium changed my perspective; it reminded me of who I was, what I was made of, and that defeat is unacceptable. This led me to create a personal development system called 4Self. The system embodies the most important characteristics that I needed to get on the road to recovery.

I invested time in myself and became dedicated to the success of my rebirth. Within weeks, there was a noticeable change—a released burden—and life was looking up. The vast improvement in my well-being not only helped me physically, mentally, and emotionally, but my career started to explode. Within a few short years, I was making six figures, owned my dream car, and life was amazing.

For the first time in almost two years, I felt at peace and living my best life. I turned my scars into victory and helped others who were struggling with similar predicaments to also live their best life.

Life is too short to not invest in yourself. Don't procrastinate what you should do today for another day. Loving you is one of the most important things you can do for yourself.

I can assure you that if you learn from my mistakes and work on 4Self daily, you will start loving yourself regardless of the setback. I have shared with you so many of the good, bad, and ugly experiences that have shaped my life. Now it's your turn to recognize your position as number one in your own life. Follow the path which led to my rebirth and experience your own renaissance.

CHAPTER 1:

Reconnection

One of the lowest points in my life was when I hit rock bottom after my business failed and I had to close it down. I was in a depressive state, but didn't realize the outward effects until my mom forced me to go to the doctor when I refused to open up about my feelings. The sadness and disappointment from losing something so important left me with an enormous void and my vulnerability was palpable. The last thing I needed to do was jump into a relationship.

This part of my life story began when I was forced to give up my baby - no not an actual human baby, but *my* baby. My high-end lingerie business meant the world to me, from design to creation, I was involved in every step of the process. But due to the high costs of my chosen fabrics and using small manufacturers in Manhattan, it just couldn't survive the financial burden. My parents invested heavily, but I was hemorrhaging money and couldn't afford to continue production with little to no return.

I then sunk into a devastating depression and the pain wasn't only emotional, it actually physically hurt like hell. It was hard to process the loss of something I worked so hard for; the loss of what I thought was my future. I was in such a dark place, somewhere so doomed that I felt no hope, no joy. Then, the unexpected happened: a blast from the past sent me an email.

I still remember staring at the computer screen, reading the email over and over, surprised by the reemergence of my old college boyfriend-Josh. The one, who, when we parted ways seven years ago, promised to find and marry me when we were older. Could this be happening? A little bit of hope in a dark valley; a chance to rekindle a love that was once shared.

I quickly responded, expressing my joy to him for reconnecting. I also included my telephone number, in the hope of encouraging a prompt reunion. After our first conversation, it was as though we hadn't missed a moment apart. Like two peas in a very comfortable pod, fitting back into a familiar routine. We caught up on our lives, talking daily, late into the night and early morning as he worked an overnight job.

I felt happy for the first time in months, and was no longer feeling the pain of depression due to the loss of my business. With my ex back in the picture, everything smelled like roses and felt like heaven. At the time, my desperate need for something good to happen - due to the failure of my business - clouded my judgment. I was vulnerable, which left me open to making rash decisions with no thought of consequences.

Our first date was at the Metropolitan Museum of Art in Manhattan. We went to see the Costume Institute exhibition, a favorite of mine. I was a ball of excitement and nerves from the time I woke up to the moment I spotted him standing on the top step of the famed museum. My thirtieth birthday was only a few months away, but my heart was racing like a pre-teen locking eyes with her crush for the first time. I was ecstatic! The belief that something good was happening to me after months of gut-wrenching pain made my heart sing and my confidence soar.

The date was blissful. He said all the right things and made all the right moves; in return, I coquettishly batted my eyelashes and life seemed perfect. Later, we enjoyed a romantic meal which I have little memory of, because by that time, I was in such a 'love bubble' that neither food nor drink mattered. Lovestruck, I didn't want the date to end - it was everything and so much more than I imagined it would be.

For weeks, then months after the initial date, we continued to have long meaningful conversations until the wee hours of the morning. We also enjoyed each other's company and went on dates as much as possible. There was no denying our chemistry and reconnecting only made it more intense. God was definitely smiling on me and I felt privileged to have Josh back in my life, even if my gut feeling didn't feel quite so positive.

Lessons Learned

1. Deal with your emotions, don't mask them.
2. Don't confuse like, lust, or love.

Chapter 2:

Don't Ignore Your Gut

One of the things about life is that so many of our choices and decisions are totally up to us. Whether we choose to admit or not, our gut instinct is usually correct and not to be ignored. However, like most things I know, it's easier said than done. Wanting something to be a certain way is usually a more powerful pull than the truth, no matter the repercussions.

By now we'd been dating for about two months and it couldn't get any better. He was the ying to my yang, my soulmate. Our love was in full bloom and the summer sun couldn't shine any brighter—or so I thought.

To change things up a little, we decided to go to Dorney Park for a day of fun and adventure. We were a threesome; my best friend Bailey, whose date canceled at the last minute, was with us. The day was light and pleasurable, until it wasn't.

After a fabulous day of rides, cotton candy and inhaling funnel cake, the drive home turned into a disaster. An argument about which direction to take back to

Brooklyn ensued between the two of us—though we weren't driving.

Looking back, it's ridiculous to think that something so minor turned really major, really quickly, but it did. Within moments, we went from a happy couple to warring partners. The anger that spewed as we made the one-hundred plus mile journey back, was palpable. Neither one of us backed down as rage-fueled vitriol permeated through the car's interior. We showed no restraint or respect for Bailey as she drove, trying to ignore our bitter soundtrack.

Arriving back in Brooklyn, Bailey dropped us off at his apartment, which I'm sure was a huge relief for her. Vexed, I clamored up the steps to the brownstone building, the tension so thick only a machete could cut through. Once inside—without the constraints of a car - the argument escalated to a heated verbal fight. So much so that, within hours, he kicked me out and told me to wait outside in the street for a ride. He was done and decided to go to the overnight job that he was on vacation from rather than to sort out the problem. What?!

I watched him head towards the subway as he left for his job, while I stood on the sidewalk in utter disbelief. How could this man who claimed he loved me, leave me outside in the dark of night on a scary Brooklyn sidewalk? However, even with that big red flag glaring in my face, I still loved him and wanted things to work out.

Thankfully, I didn't have to wait long, as Bailey, who only lived ten minutes away, came to pick me up within a half an hour. Driving back to her home, I rehashed the argument and explained how I ended up stranded outside. I was beyond pissed and still in disbelief that he could abandon me like that. Bailey, who'd known him as long as I had, was equally upset and mad at the disrespect he showed me. We were both bewildered and felt deceived by the man we'd known for almost a decade.

Shortly after our arrival, Bailey received a phone call from him claiming concern about my whereabouts. Being a good friend, she basically read him the riot act, letting him know that he messed up. Big time!

After letting him know her disappointment, she handed the phone over to me. He stated his regrets, asking for my forgiveness and I readily accepted his apology. Within hours, once he returned from work, I was back at his apartment acting as if nothing happened.

Our emotions overflowed as we greeted each other in the vestibule of the building, happy to be back together. Being in his embrace is where I wanted to be and the events of the previous night were now a far distant memory.

The rest of the day was spent watching movies and walking to the neighborhood exotic ice cream shop. While enjoying my Guinness flavored ice cream, I made a decision that changed the course of my life. As we discussed preventing a repeat of last night's behavior, a stupid idea popped into my head and instead of letting it stay there, I said it out loud.

"We should get married!" Saying the words aloud sounded even more ridiculous than the thought did in my head. Yet, surprisingly, he didn't seem fazed by my impulsive pronouncement. I explained that by doing so, we were proving that we loved each other; that the explosive and angry words spoken during our fight were only said in spite, not in truth.

"Ok," he agreed. And just like that, we made a life-changing decision without any concern about the consequences. We had decided to get married to fix an issue as if that was the answer. We attempted to put a band-aid on underlying problems instead of trying to resolve them—an absurd reason to make such an important decision… But hindsight is always clearer.

Lessons Learned

1. When someone doesn't care about your physical, emotional, or mental well-being, it's time to move on.
2. You should always feel safe and protected by loved ones.

3. There's always a price to pay for decisions made in haste.

Chapter 3:

No Way!

It's unreal to think about how I could've made such a rash decision. If anyone else told me that they did something like this, I would chide them for having bad judgment. Yet, here I am—a smart, grown woman making childish mistakes with zero awareness.

For the next few days and weeks, I floated around on a cloud of fluffiness. I was beyond elated. Here I was almost thirty years old, with the man of my dreams whom I'm about to marry. How lucky was I? Hah!

Now, when I think back, it pains me to think that I was in such a dark place and not thinking wisely.

Losing my business had more of an impact than I had expected. Regrettably, I never properly grieved the loss; instead, I buried my feelings and allowed my vulnerability to encourage stupid decisions.

I quickly decided that if I was going to get married, then I might as well keep up with the Jones' and do it at thirty. Never before has marrying at thirty been a goal of mine. Yet, suddenly, as I continued to be swept up in the wedding day (and not the actual marriage), I was determined that the nuptials had to take place before my thirty-first birthday.

This rushed timeline gave me fifteen months to plan the wedding I never dreamt of or thought I wanted. However, once I got in the groove, it actually became a fun project—like planning one of my legendary parties. After weighing tons of options, we decided on a destination wedding to Antigua in the fall of the following year. The date was set, and I had a wedding to plan.

With my sole focus on planning a fabulous day, I never took into consideration that marriage is so much more than a dress, flowers, and an elaborate menu. Conversations about our future were few and we never discussed basics such as children or religion.

Counseling was suggested and quickly dismissed. He didn't believe in going to tell a stranger about our issues, and believed that we could handle our problems privately. Fine with me, really; I didn't care to go to counseling either, and only suggested it because it was on a must-do-list in one of my bridal magazines.

After all, at that point my parents had been married over forty years and made marriage look easy. And even their prudent advice for us to go to counseling fell on deaf ears. As far as we were concerned, we knew what we were doing and didn't need or want anyone else's opinion.

Months crept by while I focused my tunnel vision on planning the perfect wedding day. I was on a roll and nothing - not even a bulldozer—could stop me. I was excited to have a wedding with the beautiful, tropical backdrop of the island, and organized each moment as if my life depended on it.

Every detail was meticulously planned, including the highly recommended photographer who I was flying in for the occasion. My dress, along with the bridesmaids' dresses, was chosen, and as the day rapidly approached, the excitement started to build.

Once again, friends and family advised us to attend counseling to resolve our issues, but like the stubborn fools we were, the answer always remained no. We didn't have a clue about what we were getting into but that didn't stop us from hurtling full-speed ahead.

At the bridal shower - which was three months before the wedding—the first wave of doubt appeared and my earlier excitement turned into apprehension. I'd been uneasy about the marriage as soon as the suggestion flew out of my mouth a year ago, but with the busyness of the wedding, I was able to bury my feelings and mask them with faux joy. Now, with just a few untied loose ends left, the reality of what I was about to embark upon hit deep down to my core.

The beautifully decorated shower is now like a fading dream to me; bits and parts of the memory surface at times, but anxiety was the enduring emotion I experienced. I plastered a smile on my face as I met some of his family for the first time, making sure to leave a good impression, while deep down all I could think was, *'What the hell am I doing?'*.

As the wedding day drew closer, I started to feel sudden waves of panic whenever the event was mentioned. But I was already in too deep; final deposits had been made, guests had their travel arrangements, and there was no turning back. At this point, I knew that I had to suck it up and proceed with my fate.

Lessons Learned

1. Don't be a follower. Doing anything for the purpose of keeping up with anyone else, will never make you happy.
2. Counseling and coaching are positive tools that can enhance any relationship.
3. Be discerning, yet open to wise advice.

Chapter 4:

I'm Getting Married!

Sometimes, reliving the memory is so hard. It's still very difficult to wrap my mind around making such a silly and impulsive decision. I wasn't one of those little girls who daydreamed about a fantasy wedding with a magical prince, nor was I an adult who dreamt about being swept away by love. So that's why it's so hard for me at times to come to grips with what I did. How could I have possibly been so foolish?

I woke up on the morning of our flight to Antigua, feeling numb. One part of me was elated to go to a beautiful island to have a fabulous party with loved ones. The other felt dread and detachment - resigned to my fate. On the way to the airport, I decided to let the stress and unnerving feelings go. I made this bed and now it was time for me to lay in it.

The luxury, all-inclusive resort was gorgeous, with expansive grounds that stretched for miles on the pristine white sand beach, Dickenson Bay. Our opulent residence for the week was a rondoval-styled bungalow with a private butler and pool. We had a couple of days to enjoy before the guests arrived for the wedding, and I was definitely going to make the most out of it.

The next day, we had fun in the sun and roamed the grounds enjoying all that it had to offer. The truth is, we weren't ready for marriage, but we had a fantastic friendship and enjoyed each other's company immensely. Later, we met with our officiant and filled out the remaining paperwork, including the marriage license. As I signed the document, the uneasy feeling I had all along resurfaced and there was no denying that I had made a mistake.

By the time our friends and family arrived, I was ready to have a party—or what I call a 'bashment'. The wedding was the following day, and everyone who came was super excited to be on the island and a part of our special day. On the outside, I was having an amazing time; surrounded by friends and family is always the place to be. But on the inside, I was dying and couldn't even express how I felt to anyone, including my best friend Bailey.

How could I tell them that I made a mistake, that I didn't want to get married? How? In my mind, I couldn't—not because they would be mad or judgmental, but more so, it would mean that I had failed. I've always been a super overachiever and failure wasn't an option as far as I was concerned. So here I was, lying to everyone I loved all due to my ego.

The morning of the wedding, I woke up and prayed to God for strength and guidance because, boy, did I need it. I went through the motions, getting my hair and makeup done, taking pictures—all the while acting like the perfect bride-to-be. My poker face was on, and I was ready to play the part.

But I wasn't fooling everyone. My mom knew something was wrong, and kept asking me what the problem was, however, I shamelessly lied to her as if it was nothing. I'd psyched myself up to do this and I was not about to give in to anyone.

As I was being helped into my dress, my heart raced and pounded uncontrollably. This was it. It was really happening; I was getting married.

In vain, I feebly pushed against my chest cavity in an attempt to slow my heart rate, but of course, nothing could stop it from racing like an out-of-control freight train. My mom shot me a final glance. Her eyes filled with concern as she knew, like only a mother could, that something was wrong. I ignored her worried glance and prepared to head towards the ceremony on the beach.

As my dad walked me down the aisle and squeezed my hand reassuringly, I did all that I could to stop from freaking out and crying like a mad woman. At that moment, the only thing I wanted to do was fall into my dad's comforting arms and bawl like a baby. Then, out of nowhere, the perfectly sunny day turned into an unexpected rainstorm. As we dove for cover, my only thought was that even heaven was crying for me!

Within minutes, the rain stopped and we proceeded with the ceremony. Like in the movies, a part of me wished that when the minister asked if there were objections, that someone would respond and save me from myself. But this wasn't a movie.

The reception, which took place in a room steps away from the outdoor ceremony was decorated with sophisticated, tropical decor. The gorgeous exotic flowers, including the magnificent bird of paradise which made up my bouquet, also festooned the tables.

While we enjoyed the cocktail hour and mingled, I noticed how unhappy my two-years-old (at the time) niece and my mom were. Though she was at that tricky 'terrible twos' age, she was usually a smiling and happy child who enjoyed being around her family, so her behavior struck me as being odd.

Could it be the spiritual sensitivity of a child? Did she sense that I was making a mistake? Maybe. On the other hand, I knew why my mom was upset; seeing me and knowing that something was wrong distressed her, which showed in her demeanor.

The reception was a blast. Delicious gourmet food and great company is always a perfect combination and to top off the night my favorite dessert, baked Alaska, was served. Everyone had a great time, and it was definitely one of the best bashments I've ever thrown.

After breakfast the next day, we bid goodbye to our guests and continued with the honeymoon. Later, we joined other couples at the resort to play the newlywed game, which was a disaster! He answered most of the questions correctly, but I failed miserably, which led to our loss. In retrospect, the game was a significant sign - not knowing important details about your spouse is a dead giveaway that there's a problem.

We enjoyed the rest of the week at the beautiful resort, mingling with new-found friends and having the time of our lives. But it was time to get back to reality and start our new life as a married couple back home on Long Island.

Lessons Learned

1. Don't suffer in silence. Talk with someone you trust when you're in crisis.
2. Lying, especially when it's just to save face, is always a bad option. The truth always comes out.

CHAPTER 5:

The Honeymoon is Definitely Over

You know when so many signs are thrown right in front of your face and you still ignore every single one of them, you really do deserve whatever happens. I totally ignored all signs, from my niece behaving out of character to my constant anxiety, and that's only the beginning. As time went by, I continued to turn a blind eye to things that were right in front of my face and I ended up paying for it all, deservingly so.

On our return, we started settling into our life together, but the problems we had previously ignored, returned. After my business dissolved, I worked odd jobs so I could continue my hustle on the side. Being an entrepreneur was all I've ever wanted to be; it's in my blood and runs deep through my veins. At the time, I was baking and looking forward to being a stagiaire at a culinary school in Manhattan, which would lead to me attending for free.

Baking is a passion of mine, but it wasn't bringing in any money and my odd jobs—when I had one—didn't contribute much, making him the sole breadwinner; a role he very quickly grew tired of and to an extent, I can't blame him for feeling that way. After all, who wants to feel like the only participant in a two-person team? On the flip side, he knew who I was. I was a struggling entrepreneur and college student when we first met over ten years ago. My passion for entrepreneurship never wavered; it's who I've always been.

That's why discussing basics—including finances, children, and religion—is so important before even thinking about marriage. And by not doing so, we did an injustice to ourselves and our hope of having a healthy union.

Our arguments were harsh and frequent and usually stemmed from money issues. Being a stagiaire bringing in no income while I pursued my culinary career, was a huge topic of contention. He felt that it was a waste and pointless career move which wouldn't really amount to anything. I just wanted him to believe in me and support my decision.

Then, to make matters worse, we were hit with another obstacle involving our photographer. A few weeks after the wedding, we received the proofs and set up a meeting to choose the pictures for the coffee table book and other albums which were included in the package price. We were supposed to receive the finished products within a few weeks after the meeting, but a month passed with no word of shipment.

I repeatedly called the company and the photographer's personal number with no response for days on end. Eventually, I heard back from someone after two weeks, who informed me that the company closed but they would be sending my package out shortly. I was surprised that the bustling office I had visited just a few weeks ago was now closed - something seemed off.

Weeks passed and I still did not receive a package. By now, no one returned my calls. However, a short time later I received an email from the State Attorney's office notifying me of a case against the studio. Evidently, they'd fleeced dozens of brides, including some who paid for the package and no photographer showed up. They asked me to provide information so they could try to retrieve my albums, as they had seized all the contents of the office.

I provided the requested information—concerned more about how my husband would react, knowing we lost thousands of dollars, than the loss of the albums. We'd paid the final deposit a few weeks ago when we met at the studio and now, we were out of everything. I felt like an idiot. The studio came highly recommended and we paid a lot of money for the pictures in addition to the photographer's airfare and hotel accommodations. This was not going to go well.

After prolonging the inevitable, I eventually told him about the email a couple of days after it was confirmed that our items were not in the office. As expected, it led to another fight about finances. We were stuck in a bad situation—in a marriage that was falling apart way before the first anniversary. But this latest setback felt like another blazing sign; we had no coffee table book, no mother-in-law albums, no frames, nothing but proofs of our wedding day. It almost felt like the wedding didn't happen.

Lesson Learned

1. Before committing to a serious relationship, discuss the things that matter most -especially the non-negotiables.

CHAPTER 6:

Emotional Affair, Whatever!

You know when people show you who they are, you mustn't ignore them; they're not lying to you. No one has the power to make someone into something they're not, unless they also want to make the change—so don't even try. When all the signs are written all over the wall, it's time to stop ignoring them and take heed.

We celebrated our first wedding anniversary a few months after the photography debacle. 'Celebrated' is a generous term. Midway through dinner at the fancy restaurant we chose for our anniversary meal, an argument ensued—this time over perceived flirting between me and the waiter. This did not happen, but our marriage had become that pitiful, and we were both to blame. We constantly stoked the flames, provoking one another in hopes of some kind of reaction. At this rate, it was only a matter of time before someone blew.

A month after our anniversary, we were preparing to have our first Christmas together as husband and wife. Then a few days before Christmas, he came home from his company work party where he had been drinking heavily. He laid down and fell asleep within minutes. I laid down beside him, unable to sleep because I felt rejected by our non-existent love life.

The constant pinging of his cell phone started to annoy me after a while. He was sleeping so heavily that he didn't even stir, so I eventually got out of the bed and walked around to his side to mute the horrid sound. However, when I picked up the phone, it 'woke up' the screen, enabling the backlight. And what I read on the screen sent my body into panic and blood rushing to my head.

With my hand shaking and heart racing, I took the phone into the bathroom and looked at the screen again. On it was a text exchange between my husband and his 'sweetie'. He told her that he came by her house after his office party, but she didn't answer the door. He said that he missed her and wanted to see her. He signed off declaring his longingness for them to see each other again.

She responded by telling him that he could come over now, and how sorry she was to have missed him. I was floored, gobsmacked, and in total disbelief; it felt as if someone had literally taken my breath away.

I read the text a few more times, and then stormed back into the bedroom and threw the phone at his head while yelling at him, asking who this woman was.

Startled from his deep sleep, it took him a few seconds to realize what was happening while I continued to scream at him, demanding answers.

As he scrambled to gather his thoughts, I grabbed the phone back and dialed her number. She answered immediately, asking how her 'sweetie' was doing. Before he could utter a word, I let her know in quite colorful language that she was talking to his wife. Nonplussed by my assertion, she called out to him on the speaker, telling him to 'control his crazy wife'. Wow.

My heart sunk when those words came out of her mouth; it was confirmation that they had something going on. It meant that he talked about me and she felt comfortable enough to say those hurtful words. My brain whirled as I heard him quickly try to calm her down and disconnect the call. I knew things weren't good between us, but I didn't think we had hit such a low. The realization that he was having an affair was devastating.

He spoke first, trying to convince me that it was 'only an emotional affair, nothing serious'. What? I'd never even heard of an emotional affair until that moment. I just sat on the edge of the bed feeling confused with my heart torn into pieces and tears rolling down my face. I really couldn't believe what was happening. I'd been in denial for so long, now reality was slapping me harder than I could handle.

I yelled at him through tears, screaming at him, asking why and how he could do this to us, to our marriage. In return, I received a variety of basic responses from he didn't have sex with her, to he's sorry, to it won't happen again. Weakened by my underlying depression and not wanting my marriage to fail, I eventually gave in to his promise to make things better.

It was the early morning before I stopped crying, with him reassuring me that things would change. We then got back into bed for a couple of hours before waking up to start our day.

I woke up with swollen eyes from hours of crying and a pit deep in my stomach—no, I did not dream the events of last night; it actually happened. As he rushed off to go to work, I started my day in a daze. The lack of trust that I now felt and the blow to my ego was stifling. How could I agree to continue on in a relationship where I felt no trust and totally worn down?

But I did. I stayed and hoped that we would be able to work it out. There was no way that I would consider defeat, so I had to stay. I had to save my marriage, no matter how empty it made me feel or how low my self-esteem dipped.

Lessons Learned

1. Don't ignore it when people show their true selves. Just because we don't like what we see, doesn't mean it's not true. Pay attention.
2. Never stay in a relationship that tears down your self-worth and self-esteem.
3. If there's no trust, there's no marriage.

CHAPTER 7:

We're Done!

It's crazy how easy it is to convince yourself of something that's not true - basically like gaslighting yourself. But in all fairness, sometimes our instinct to protect ourselves from a harsh reality is a way of softening the blow, making it easier to cope. The problem is that you can't stay in denial forever. At some point, the facts become the greater reality and there's nowhere to hide from the truth.

The last year had been painful and knowing that he had an 'emotional' affair left me in a constant state of distrust. Since culinary school was such a topic of contention, I ended up quitting shortly after the revelation. A couple of months later, I enrolled in a skin care program and became a licensed aesthetician.

Fourteen months after discovering his affair, I landed a job close to home—not in skin care, but in customer service for an insurance company. At this point, I wasn't picky. I knew my marriage was in danger of collapsing and I was willing to do whatever it took to make it work. The new job gave me a sense of accomplishment and eventually, I was able to be a substantial contributor to our team. But the bombs hadn't finished dropping.

Receiving my first paycheck in over a year filled me with such a feeling of contentment. Money was our biggest issue, and now that I was bringing in a decent sized check, our marriage was saved! Or so I thought. The first thing that I wanted to do was take my husband out for dinner—now that I could pay for it - to show appreciation for his patience. So, I made a date for us to go out on Saturday night to a local steakhouse.

That day, I woke up feeling so good, so excited for the night ahead. He was in Brooklyn visiting family and we were all set for an 8 pm dinner date. As the time drew closer, I took my time getting dressed, making sure to look my best. I was taking my man out to dinner and I wanted to make him want me again. This was our first date in a long time, and it had to be perfect.

He arrived home about fifteen minutes before our reservation, seemingly unfazed by our dinner date. I reminded him of the time and expressed that we needed to leave immediately. By his lack of concern, I knew there was a problem. As usual, I chose to ignore it. I had planned diligently for the night and nothing was going to screw it up, whatever his problem was, he'd get over it once we were out having a good time. Right!

We made small talk during the ten-minute drive to the restaurant, but the tension was undeniably thick. Though he didn't have much to say, he had a sense of happiness on his face, a joy that I hadn't seen in a while. He was smiling and it was obvious that he had made a decision that he was at peace about.

Seated at our table, I knew that I couldn't avoid the elephant in the room any longer and asked him what the problem was. He responded that everything was good, but it didn't take a genius to figure out that he wanted to be anywhere but there with me.

We continued with small talk while looking through the menu, but my gut indicated that there was a major problem. I could feel it and my subconscious knew what it was, but I couldn't get the words out. I didn't want to admit the inevitable until I had to. But deep down, I knew he wasn't going to say it; so eventually, I did. I asked him if he was leaving me. And just like that, my world crumbled as he coldly and quickly answered 'yes'.

I sat at the table stunned, unable to form a response. Bells started ringing in my head and I immediately felt faint then the waterworks came in full force. I couldn't control myself. I was seated at a table in a busy restaurant, crying my eyes out—beyond devastated and broken. I heard what he said, but my brain and heart couldn't accept it. I was a wreck. I could not believe he was ending our marriage right there in the restaurant.

The waiter came by to take our order, and when he noticed my tear-stricken face, said that he would come back. As I sat at the table across from my husband quietly sobbing, he didn't even attempt to comfort me. He just sat there picking at the bread on the table, his face smug with satisfaction. I knew by looking at him that he was already over it.

We left the restaurant without ordering. I couldn't possibly sit there any longer, feeling so humiliated. I ignored the stares as I walked out, still upset. I didn't care if anyone saw me crying; the only thing that mattered at that moment was the fact that he was leaving me. In the car ride home, I begged him not to leave. I said that I could do better, I could be better. I promised anything he wanted, as long as he stayed, but he was having none of it.

Back home, he told me that he was moving out the following day, a Sunday, and would not be back. My mind raced as I tried to take it all in, tried to digest my new reality, but I couldn't. I could not grasp what was happening; it was just too much.

That night, we went to bed together for the last time after my incessant pleas for him to reconsider failed to change his mind. It was so weird lying beside the person who just ripped my heart out like nothing happened. My tears constantly flowed as my body laid numb. He tried to reassure me that it was for the best.

He said we weren't happy and deserved to be, so we had to part.

I woke up to him packing his clothes. I couldn't believe how relaxed he was about the situation. He almost seemed giddy—excited for his new life. After staring at him for what seemed like an eternity, but was in reality maybe only thirty seconds, I got out of the bed and headed to the bathroom. I felt sick to my stomach, still in disbelief that my marriage was over.

When I went back into the bedroom, he casually asked me how I was doing, as if he didn't know how the hell I felt! His complacent attitude added even more fuel to the well-lit fire. I was so broken that I lacked the strength to fight fire with more fire and ignored him instead. Deep down, I just continued to sink into a dark hole of hurt, disbelief, and pain.

I watched as he made numerous trips to his truck, packing up all his belongings, and within a few hours, he was finished. Stepping back inside the house, he made his final run-through before walking over to where I stood by the window. He told me how much he always loved me and in fact, believed that he loved me more than I loved him.

And though it sounds cheesy, there's truth in his words. I made a vow to never love again at nine years old during my move to Jamaica, and held steadfast to it. Yes, I cared about him—maybe even had a slight infatuation—but it took me a couple of years to admit that I never loved him.

Then he went on to stress that we should remain friends with the chance of us reuniting once again when our lives were in a better place. The glimmer of hope warmed my heart a little. I didn't know it then, but he was only selling me a dream—a really crap one at that.

Then, with a hug and kiss, he was gone. Watching him drive down the street, my inner self cried out for him to turn around, but he kept going and I felt destroyed. Within a few minutes, I made my first phone call to Bailey, whom I hadn't spoken to since leaving for dinner the previous night. Her shock at my revelation was evident; she seemed almost as surprised as I was.

Saying out loud that my marriage was over was one of the hardest things I've ever said, and it hurt like hell. I still couldn't believe my new reality and was hoping to wake from the nightmare as soon as possible.

I told my parents next, after they arrived home from church. That hurt the most, explaining that he had walked out on me was embarrassing and hurtful, but I also felt like such a disappointment with a failed marriage after only two years. However, my parents' loving reaction removed all doubt of them being displeased with me.

After positive and supportive responses from my loved ones, I began to feel a tad bit better. However, I knew that the bigger test would be when I had to go to work the following day. I planned to act like everything was normal, that I had an uneventful weekend. I'd only been at the job for a few weeks and did not want anyone to think that my work would suffer if they knew my situation. Tomorrow would be the biggest acting job of my life, and I was ready for the role.

Lesson Learned

1. Denial gets you nowhere.

CHAPTER 8 :

Back at the J.O.B.

There were so many times that I wished I had the superpower of invisibility. With my life crumbling to pieces, it was hard to face the world as if all was good. But I did. For weeks and months, I lied to those who I was just getting to know and forbade my immediate family and friends from telling anyone else. To put it mildly, I was ashamed, and did not want to tell the truth when I couldn't even accept it.

The day after D-day (departure day) was horrible. I thought I was ready to play the role of a lifetime, but little can prepare you for that aching feeling of love and loss. At work, while everyone discussed the events of their weekend, I hoped to make myself invisible and stayed out of the mix. I busied myself with work and avoided small talk as much as possible. My new normal was avoidance and being incognito.

The customer calls became a form of solace. I was able to lose myself in their issues, allowing me to forget about my own, if only momentarily. I thanked God that I had a distraction for eight hours every day, but dreaded the weekends when I had forty-eight hours to think nonstop about my predicament.

Every day, the pain felt so intense that I didn't think it would ever dissipate. I felt like I was living a real-life version of the movie, *Groundhog Day*. Every. Single. Day. Most days, we called each other and argued, further prolonging the anguish and pain. Sometimes, the hateful and angry vitriol was so bitter that I had to retreat to the bathroom to release my tears, not wanting my coworkers to notice my sorrow.

I was in a constant state of grief and did not believe that I could get out of it. My depression was at an all-time low, and holding the secret so close to my cuff was wearing me thin. I was in a bad place and didn't know what to do about it, but I still held out hope that he would reconsider, which would allow me to wake from this maddening horror show.

To add insult to injury, I blamed myself entirely for the separation. I believed that I didn't do enough to work on the marriage and regretted not being a better wife. My self-esteem was at such a negative level that I made him totally blameless while dragging myself through the mud. The guilt and regret weighed heavily on my mind and I only wanted to make things right again.

The hardest part was answering questions about Josh. I had become friendly with some of my coworkers and hanging out as a couple was a constant hot topic.

Instead of admitting my truth, I lied and made excuses for him avoiding the prospect of weekend 'double dating'.

However, after a few weeks, I decided to put my trust in a coworker who sat at the desk closest to me. We talked constantly, and it was becoming increasingly difficult to keep the lie going. To my surprise, her reaction was filled with concern and no judgment. She promised not to share my secret with anyone, and soon became a great friend, which she still is to this day.

Though I felt awful for tangling her into my web of lies, her loyalty and friendship were more than appreciated. I still believed that our marriage could be saved, so I held back from dishing the unflattering details of our union.

It was refreshing to receive feedback from a neutral party who didn't know much about our history— including our abysmal rush to the altar. She, like my other family and friends who were privy to the situation, was a rock star during my darkest days, and that is something I will never forget.

Lessons Learned

1. We are usually our own harshest critics. Ease up a little.
2. Lying is always a bad idea, but more so when you involve an innocent party.

Chapter 9:

It's Your Fault!

Ok, I know I've said this before, but because it's so important to stress, I'm going to say it again. If someone, especially a significant other, tells you who they are or what they do/don't want, believe them! I couldn't accept the hard truth that Josh did not want to save the marriage, so, in turn, I begged for something to happen that was not going to happen. In the process, my already fragile self-esteem took a nosedive. I ignored what was clearly in front of my face, instead, choosing to believe that I could fix the unfixable.

A month after the separation, I convinced Josh after weeks of begging, to go to couples' therapy. Though he reluctantly obliged, I believed that once we attended the sessions, all of our problems would be resolved. After foolishly declining premarital counseling, I was determined to succeed this time around.

On the day of the appointment, he picked me up, and I was so happy to see him. I wanted nothing more than to be reunited and have a happy life together. I broke the ice by telling him that Poochie, my gorgeous Chihuahua / Shih Tzu mix who he's known since my college days, missed him. He barely cracked a smile upon hearing that and abruptly warned me that going to the session did not mean he wanted me back. Yeah, that definitely hurt right in the gut, but I brushed it off, still believing that the therapy would resolve our issues.

The session started out with the therapist introducing herself and explaining her role. As we answered questions about our marriage, she abruptly stopped us from talking to tell us what she'd decided. Supposedly, I was the problem in the relationship and would, therefore, need to start private appointments before any further couple sessions. Yikes!

What could possibly be worse? Well, it was bad enough that this alleged professional made such a pronouncement after only a few minutes of speaking to me. Of course, her decision gave Josh the satisfaction he relished. After the session was over, he gleefully taunted me with 'I told you so's' and 'I told you it was your fault', all the while beaming with pride as we walked back to his car. His cheeriness at the expense of my hurt feelings was the final kick to my dying self-esteem.

The following week, I went to my first and last one-on-one session with the therapist. After talking through some early childhood memories, our time was almost up. Relieved, I listened as she offered her supposedly sage advice and decided then that it would be my last appointment. Her session, which was meant to be a tool to figure out the issues in our marriage, turned into a slugfest about my personality.

What's really sad is that I was in such a deep, dark, and helpless place that I couldn't even stand up for myself as I would've ordinarily done. I allowed this person, who barely knew me, to make biased judgments about my character. My self-esteem was shot and my self-respect wasn't far behind. I was tunneling deeper into a depressive abyss and didn't understand the depths of my own sadness.

Lessons Learned

1. For counseling to work, all participants must be willing to learn.
2. The breakdown of a marriage is a joint effort—not solo, regardless of what some may say.

CHAPTER 10:

It Hurts So Bad

Sometimes, when I think back to how desperate I was to save my marriage, I cringe. What's worse is the fact that it was more about an ego trip rather than trying to be with someone I supposedly loved. I was so intent on 'saving face' that I lost all perspective and become someone I didn't even recognize. I was obsessed with winning and would go to all lengths, all extremes, to not lose the biggest game of my life. I was out of control and beyond reason.

The failed therapy sessions left me feeling dejected and in total despair. If that didn't work, what the hell would? I knew I had to do something else, but right now I had more important issues to deal with, which thankfully, gave me a mini-break from the everyday focus of reuniting with Josh.

My beautiful and loyal Poochie who had been with me from her birth fourteen years ago, was very ill with congestive heart failure. I was inconsolable. She'd been on medication for almost a year and contrary to what I hoped, she was not going to get better.

My final days with her were filled with love and family, and though I repeatedly pleaded with her not to leave me, I knew that her body was tired and sick and she was ready to pass. She had been a such a rock since the separation, snuggling with me even more when she felt my sadness. But her duty on earth was complete and it was time for her to go and play over the rainbow bridge.

The night she passed, I called Josh to let him know about her death. He gave his half-hearted condolences, but I could tell that his mind was miles away. He really didn't seem to care at all. Then I heard her voice in the background, talking and laughing to him as he feebly attempted to continue our conversation. I could've died just hearing their jovial exchange over the phone, but thankfully, it didn't last long as he told me he had company and had to go.

Hanging up, I realized something that I had been fighting to admit since D-day. He had moved on. He had moved on and sounded as carefree and jolly as only someone who had moved on from their marriage could. Even with these realities slapping me in the face, I still believed that there was hope; hope that he would come to his senses and realize that he did want to mend the fence.

A few more months passed and though it was getting easier to cope with being separated, the pain still hurt immensely. Losing Poochie also added so much to the pain. Some days I didn't know what hurt more. I was truly stuck in a rut, but I had one bit of fortune on my side—my job; I knew for a fact that without it, I would have fallen deeper, if that's even possible.

Around this time, we started to talk sporadically and even agreed to attend the Mets newest Costume Institute exhibit. I was giddy with delight. I knew that soon enough, he would come around. I believed that this trip down memory lane would be the ultimate fix.

As the day approached, I became more excited with the prospect of us being together again. My hopes were high and I longed for the day when we would be side-by-side as husband and wife again. No matter how much distrust, hurt, and pain I felt since the affair revelation, the only thing I wanted, was to work it out with Josh and make my marriage a success.

The exhibit, *The Model as Muse: Embodying Fashion* was fantastic, with beautiful imagery and silhouettes on display all through the venue. But what was even more impressive was seeing him, looking as dapper as ever. This man, who I've known for so long, still had the ability to put a genuine smile on my face. I was beyond ecstatic to see him, even if he seemed a little more reserved than I would've liked.

We walked around the exhibit admiring the artwork and making small talk, while I snuck glances at him. The ease that we once had, had definitely shifted. Though I was still in denial, I couldn't ignore the heaviness of our energy. I felt desperate by the situation. This was my chance to get him back, and it didn't appear to be working. His vibe towards me was very restrained and I wondered why he agreed to meet.

Outside the museum, we talked some more before we walked to my car, which was parked a few blocks away. In my desperation, I asked him if he thought we could work things out and be a couple again. He reminded me that he only wanted to be friends, and if I couldn't do that, then we shouldn't meet up again. *Yikes!*

Ignoring his clear rejection, I continued to question if we could maybe try again at a later time, if not now. I could see him thinking about his answer, and then he surprised me by saying, "Yes, maybe at a later time we could be together again". I was euphoric. His resignation gave me all the hope I needed to believe that our lives would be united once more. After all, neither of us had taken the step to petition for divorce as yet. We were merely separated.

At my car, as we said our goodbyes, I reached in for a kiss, which he quickly rebuffed with that that 'friends, remember?' look. *Ouch*. I got in my car, sinking low into the seat – defeated. I was disappointed that the day didn't go as I imagined. I truly believed that the nostalgia of being at the museum would evoke warm memories for him, arousing a need to reunite, but I most certainly misjudged the situation.

A couple of days passed with me feeling in the dumps again, but I quickly reinvigorated myself and my mission to get Josh back. *Noooooo*. Two weeks after the disastrous exhibit date, I reached out to him again. My new plan was to be his *friend*—as he insisted—until it turned into something more. We chatted about normal stuff, basically shooting the breeze, and ended up having a decent conversation.

The next time I called, I casually brought up hanging out together at his new place in the Bronx. To my surprise, he agreed. I was pleasantly shocked and totally overjoyed. But my delight didn't last long. After asking for his address, he told me he'd give me the street address, but not the apartment number, as he didn't want me to just show up out of the blue. At that point, I didn't really care. I was just so happy, believing that we were heading in the right direction.

A week later, I asked him if I could come by, hang out, and watch movies - something that we both enjoyed doing. He told me that he already made plans for the weekend and wouldn't be home, but maybe another time. I didn't believe that he was busy so I decided to do something so cringeworthy…

That Saturday at around seven in the evening, I decided to go over to his place. I didn't believe that he was going anywhere, and decided to make an unannounced visit. I parked across the street from his building alongside a park, and called him. Obviously, I didn't have his apartment number, so I needed him to answer, which he didn't.

It was a balmy summer evening; the car air conditioner was on full blast, and I just needed him to pick up the phone. I'd been calling his number repeatedly like a raving lunatic since I arrived, and couldn't understand why—even if he wasn't at home - he couldn't answer his cell phone. Hours passed, and he still hadn't picked up. By now, the summer evening was turning dark and slightly chilly.

I continued to hunker down, sipping sparingly on my bottled water, and trying to fight the urge to use the bathroom. At no time during the whole night did I think that what I was putting myself through was beyond crazy and showed a complete lack of respect for myself and even for Josh. At some point, I fell asleep and picked up calling him when I awoke around 7 am.

Yes, I spent the entire night in my car outside Josh's house in the summer heat. Trust me I know, *cray, cray*! Eventually, he answered, and I told him I was outside and wanted to see him. He refused and questioned why I was there at that time in the morning. After explaining my bizarre behavior, I pleaded with him to let me in. I couldn't hold it in anymore.

Thankfully, he agreed, and as I used the bathroom, I started to realize what I'd done, and who I had become.

Disappointment washed over me. I was out of control and had lost respect for myself.

I was in such desperation to mend our union so I wouldn't have to tell the truth. For nearly two years, I lied to most people about being separated and burdened few to keep my secret. If I couldn't fix it, I would soon have to admit defeat and tell the truth.

I walked back to my car with a heavy heart; sad that I disrespected myself, but more upset that my plan wasn't working. I was in such a low place where I didn't love myself enough to respect who I was at the core, to be honest with myself, and say, "let it go; he doesn't want you anymore." I didn't love myself enough to be done with the games, heal from the hurt, and move on with my life.

My need to get my marriage back on track and 'win' was so out of control that I lost myself. My ego was bruised and I couldn't accept failure, which led me to put sole focus on something that—if I was honest—I would admit that I no longer wanted.

I didn't want to be married to him anymore. I just wanted to have the final say, and in the process of trying to win, I ripped my self-love, self-esteem, self-respect, and self-care to shreds. When you don't know—or forget—who you are and have no boundaries, it's easy to lack self-respect. Just like I did.

Lessons Learned

1. Don't hold onto someone who is not holding on to you.
2. Always respect yourself. Don't lose yourself and your self-respect in a relationship.
3. Dogs are man's best friend. :) (To be honest, this was not a new lesson. I've always known this!).

CHAPTER 11:

Rebirth—Part One

Whoever coined the phrase, 'hindsight is 20/20 vision' deserves a medal, because it is truly one of the realest things ever said. Looking back at all the nonsense I subjected myself to just to prove a point, was asinine. With the worst offense, no doubt being my latest, having a slumber party in my car outside of Josh's apartment building—ay! I became a shell of myself, an unrecognizable figure. If I hadn't done this stuff to myself, I wouldn't even believe it; you really can't make this crap up. That's why it was time to change the program and sing a new tune, get my soul back in check and act like I had some sense.

After the last disaster—me stalking Josh overnight - I decided to take a step back and focus more on myself and less on saving a union that was damaged beyond repair. It was hard to admit, and deep down I knew it was true, but I still had a hard time accepting his detachment to the situation. It bothered me that he didn't want our marriage to work when I, on the other hand, wanted it to work so badly—even if it was for my ego. But right now, I needed 'me' time to get my mind right before I could decide what to do about us.

As with everything I tackle in life, I went hard immediately. I started working out every day, eating better, and overachieving at work. I was on a mission to be the best me for me. But that's not really the truth. I did want to be the best me, but it wasn't as much for me as it was to show Josh, "look at me, I'm who you want".

Nonetheless, over the next few weeks and months, I continued progressing, healing mind, body, and soul. The more I worked on myself - even if the motivation was twisted - the more I started to feel like myself again. My spirit was finally on the road to renewal. I talked to Josh a couple of times after the incident, but the more I worked on myself, the less I wanted to speak to him. I could finally admit that my almost two-year obsession was moronic and totally vapid with no winners in sight.

Feeling so proud of myself with my turnaround, I planned a solo trip to Belgium for my upcoming birthday in December. Funnily, one of the reasons for my choice was because Josh and I both fell in love with a quaint town called Bruges, after watching one of our favorite movies, *In Bruges*. The other reason was because of my love of chocolate - European in particular. My itinerary was set and I couldn't wait to go on my solo expedition throughout the beautiful country.

Lesson Learned

1.   Don't allow your ego to dictate your path.

CHAPTER 12:

Belgium

I've always loved traveling, especially doing it solo. Having the freedom to do whatever, whenever is very appealing and always left me feeling liberated. With the insanity of the past twenty months, it was due time to get out on my own and feel alive again. I had caused and allowed a lot of unnecessary heartbreak during the separation and it was time to get my life back together and refocus my energy. I was about to embark on an adventure which I knew would have a massive impact on my present and future.

It had been almost two years since that dreadful evening at the steakhouse when Josh said he was done with the marriage, crushing my heart into pieces. But now, my life was in an upswing and I'd never felt better. I was promoted out of customer service and doing very well at my job at the insurance company. Taking the time to work on me was the best remedy, and I finally began to feel like my old self.

So much so that I decided to tell the truth about my separation. I started with a co-worker who always asked to double date with Josh and I. The more I repeated the story, the more at ease I felt about the decision. All of the ridiculous assumptions I had of how people would react, were unfounded; no one judged me negatively and I was reminded that I had an amazing support system.

Two months later, in December, I embarked on what would become a life altering solo trip to Belgium, starting in Brussels. After the short ride from the airport, the taxi pulled up to my hotel and I hopped out, luggage in tow, ready to get going. Feeling the energy of the nearby city center, I looked forward to exploring what it had to offer.

Traveling on my own was an experience I truly enjoyed. I recommend solo travel to everyone! The peace of being on my own, having my own schedule, and doing all the things I wanted to do, may seem daunting to some; but for me, it meant the world. I hurriedly checked in and dropped my bags off in my cozy room before I headed back outside to roam my new surroundings.

By now, it was lunchtime. Feeling famished, my first mission was to grab something to eat at a nearby restaurant which I included in my intensive itinerary. I ordered a Belgian classic, moules-frites, and people-watched while waiting on my order. It was refreshing to be in a new environment, feeling stress-free, and just enjoying life, especially after the drama of the last couple of years.

Later that evening, after taking a quick nap and unpacking my belongings, I headed back out. This time I took in the wonderful stands at the expansive Brussels Christmas market. I indulged in mulled wine and hot off the oven waffles to keep me warm. Then I watched with glee as the Grand Place lit up into a magnificent light show, robust colors lighting up every inch of the spectacular edifices - it was a breathtaking sight to behold.

The following morning, after some well-needed rest due to my jet lag, I started the day with breakfast at my hotel before I headed out to make chocolate. As most people who know me would tell you, I have a serious sweet tooth, particularly for European chocolate. So, what better way to embrace that love than to learn from the best?

Stepping into Zaabars Chocolate Factory was like entering the holy realm of exotic and exquisite chocolate. With flavors ranging from Jamaican allspice pepper to Sri Lankan lemongrass, there was something to tantalize even the most discerning taste buds. The workshop was fantastic. I made truffles and mendiants with various flavors and toppings, and had one of the best days of my life.

Being creative has always been a huge part of who I am, but after D-day I neglected myself—mind, body, and spirit. I rejected the things that once gave me peace and purpose. However, having the ability to flex those muscles to create chocolate after not being creative for so long, felt amazing. I felt refreshed and knew that this trip would bring about my rebirth.

The following day, I traveled by train through the picturesque Flemish region outside Brussels, making a short stop in Ghent before heading to Bruges. The scenic ride was so relaxing, allowing me to meditate on my blessings. I was so thankful to be in such a beautiful country, removed from all the stress of previous months.

In Bruges, I visited many of the landmarks from the movie before heading to the Christmas market. There, I indulged in more mulled wine and yummy chocolate treats. The day was everything and so much more than I could have ever thought; it was the fulfillment of a dream that Josh and I once imagined, but only I was fortunate enough to experience.

Then, it was my birthday. I enjoyed a lovely meal by myself until I met a fellow traveler, also from America. One of the many advantages of traveling solo is being more open to meeting different people. Oftentimes when traveling in a group, you feel less inclined to mingle with those outside of your circle; but when traveling solo, that doesn't necessarily apply.

My new friend and I hung out for the rest of the evening until the early morning hours, eating, drinking, and doing karaoke at a nearby neighborhood karaoke joint. By no means a tourist trap, this karaoke bar was filled with locals who embraced us warmly, and after a few hours, I felt like one of the regulars.

I had the best time ever, screeching out to Jammin' by Bob Marley while some of the locals sang background for me. I had so much fun that night, that I ended up going back the following evening. This decision would end up being the determining factor for me in taking the big step towards finalizing my divorce.

I spent my last day in Brussels eating more amazing food, walking through the city center, and shopping for chocolate. That night, after packing my bags, I went back to the karaoke bar after having such a fabulous time the night before. Most of the regulars who I had gotten to know, were there again, and we did another rendition of Jammin', with the whole bar joining in. It was amazing.

Around one in the morning, after saying goodbye to everyone and promising to return to visit, I left the bar to go back to my hotel. This entire trip had been an emotional wake-up call for me, and that night, as I walked back to my hotel, I felt exhilarated.

Walking down the dimly lit street, an overwhelming feeling of freedom came over me and the only way I could respond was to yell out 'I'm done!'. Thankfully, at that time in the morning, I was alone in the street, except for a handful of people who paid me no mind. I continued to loudly scream 'I'm done!' a few more times before exhaling for the first time in a very long time.

The power of those words as I screamed them out, released the last hold I had on saving my marriage and being with Josh. I was done with it all and looking forward to going back to New York, refreshed, rejuvenated, and over it!

Lesson Learned

1. Traveling solo is one of the best remedies for heartbreak.

Chapter 13:

Aftermath

I felt so blessed returning to New York from Belgium. I'd gone through so much adversity and felt thankful for all the lessons learned. I was in love with myself again, and happy to let go of the self-destructive mentality that had taken me down a dark path. Now that I was putting myself back together, I knew that it was time to make the final step, since Josh wasn't going to. I didn't want to live in this 'separated' bubble forever. I wanted it to be over. For real.

It felt so good to be back home. I was invigorated and ready to put in the work to build back what I would later coin, 4Self—self-love, self-esteem, self-respect, and self-care. My personal development had taken a huge hit and I knew that the only way to continue growing in a positive manner was to be consistent. I was done with trying to rebuild my marriage. I had accepted the failure and was now ready to move forward.

I no longer needed to lie about the demise of our marriage or feel ashamed because I was separated. I was moving in a new direction and it felt right. I returned to work on such a high, reflective about my amazing trip, and excited for my future. Then something happened that nearly put me back in a bad space.

I received a call from the pharmacy after I dropped off a prescription, informing me that I need a new insurance card on file, since I didn't have one. Knowing that I had insurance through Josh's job, I called the pharmacist to sort out the problem and soon realized that he had removed me from his insurance without warning. I knew that I wouldn't be able to stay on his insurance forever, but I thought he would at least have told me in advance or waited until the divorce.

I was upset and frustrated by the situation, but thankfully, I was able to get on my company's insurance immediately. I was grateful that I didn't have to beg him to reconsider and realized then that I was completely finished with him. He had obviously moved on completely and it was time for me to do the same. My next step reflected that.

The following day, I went to the courthouse and filed for an uncontested divorce. It was without a doubt one of the best days since it all began, almost two years ago. At home, I filled out the paperwork and sent him the documents that he needed to sign. Even though he was the one who left, I filed and paid for the divorce in full, and it felt great! I was finally rid of him, and couldn't wait to receive the documents back so I could officially submit them.

A week or so later, he sent the documents back to me, but they were filled out incorrectly. Trying my best to not make him get back under my skin, I returned the documents with clear instructions on how they should be completed. He didn't do the leg work, and he wasn't paying for it, so the least he could do was to fill it in correctly. I was resolved to end the marriage after trying for so long to save it, so it didn't matter how difficult he was going to be; one way or another it was going to get done.

Eventually, nearly a month after sending the paperwork, I had it back from him in the correct format and went to court on my lunch break to file the documents. After presenting the file clerk with all of my documents, I left the courthouse feeling joyous and accomplished. I was taking back my power and moving upward and onward.

The only unfortunate part was the loss of a friendship. When we met all those years ago in college, we were the best of friends before it progressed to something more. We genuinely enjoyed each other's company and trusted one another with our innermost thoughts. Due to the volatile nature of our separation, there was no door left open to rekindle the friendship, I preferred it that way. Sometimes, doors are better left closed.

A few months later, I received the notice that I had been waiting for. My divorce was finalized and I immediately felt the fabled weight lift off my shoulders. My life was now in a good place and this divorce decree was the final document to prove it. I was relieved to close this chapter and looked forward to my new one.

Lessons Learned

1. Never be ashamed of the truth; it will always set you free.
2. Tying up loose ends aids the recovery process.

CHAPTER 14:

Rebirth—Part Two!

One of the things that I was so grateful for during the separation, was the ability to go to work and forget about my personal drama for eight hours. My job became a hideaway zone; a place of solace where I could leave all the craziness behind. At the same time, there were three other coworkers who were going through a divorce, which quickly bonded us as we were able to create a support system. Moving on was something I should have done from the beginning, but I'm thankful that I realized that before it was too late.

When I received my finalized divorce paperwork, I felt as though my world was beginning to move in the right direction for the first time in a long time. I had a new lease on life. It's truly amazing how a piece of paper can make such an impact; my only regret was not doing it sooner.

With the leaps and bounds that I was making at my job, I put my entrepreneurism on the back burner. At this point, I craved stability and unfortunately, starting my own business couldn't provide that. Timing is everything, and I knew that it wasn't feasible right now. But it would be at a later date.

While my personal life suffered during the separation, my professional life soared. I started at the company over two years ago as a customer service representative and now, I was heading up my own department which I built from scratch with the Chief Operating Officer.

Within three years of the divorce, I was making six figures and living a life that I couldn't have imagined during the dark days of the separation. I never allowed my personal life to interfere with my job. In fact, I worked even harder, which made me prouder of my accomplishments.

I learned so many lessons during the last two-plus years and I'm glad for each and every one of them, no matter how many times I humiliated myself. I neglected who I was, what I stood for, and how I was raised to became someone I didn't recognize - a shell of myself. I belittled my very essence and seemed to care more about Josh than I did about my own well-being, just to protect my massive ego.

I fell all the way to the bottom, then clawed myself back up through God's grace and mercy. I knew from the beginning that the only way to rebuild my life was to create a system that would help to heal my battered mind, body, and soul.

Since I was child, I was blessed by both nature and nurture in being secure, confident and a leader. So, when I overlooked those attributes and became the opposite of what I stood for, I quickly referenced the phrase my dad encouraged my siblings and me with, and started picking up the pieces.

You're Number One was the perfect daily mantra to help refocus my energy on me. It's so important to understand that putting yourself first is vital to your everyday day growth and well-being. When you say you're number one and believe it, you make better choices, because you love and respect yourself. Also, keep in mind that sometimes it's best to fake it until you make it; so, if you don't feel like you're number one, still say it and keep saying it until you start to believe and live it.

Inspired by my daily mantra and the areas that I knew I depleted, I created the 4Self system to boost my personal development. My self-love, self-esteem, self-respect, and self-care were all at drastic lows after D-day, so 4Self was created to whip me back into shape, and it sure did!

Lessons Learned

1. Never neglect your 4Self.
2. Patience is a most worthy virtue.

CHAPTER 15:

What is 4Self?

4Self is a system I created to empower and encourage personal development, especially after a setback. I was inspired to create this system after going through the divorce and realizing how broken it made me.

Just admitting my brokenness was a shock to my system, considering how strong I've always been through any situation. However, I knew that I needed to build myself back up and used the principles that are now the basis for 4Self to do so.

4Self is about harnessing the four major attributes needed to permit yourself to invest in a better you for the well-being of your personal development. It's broken down into four principles, Self-Love, Self-Respect, Self-Esteem and Self-Care.

Daily attention of at least 15 minutes daily is required, and should be noted in a journal. In total, that's only an hour of your time per day. Having to notate that you worked on each of these areas every day gives you accountability and more importantly, a wonderful feeling of accomplishment as you see progress.

Be diligent and follow through on this as long as you need to, or as a boost whenever required. It should not be a chore to take care of yourself, so enjoy it and let it become a part of your daily routine. The more disciplined you are, the faster you'll notice the changes in how you see yourself, and with a new mindset, any goal is attainable.

Self-Love

According to *Merriam-Webster* Self-love is defined as:

a: conceit
b: regard for one's own happiness or advantage

The first definition is obviously not what I'm referring to, but it's wise to note. Self-love at the extreme can switch to conceit, so be mindful not to cross that thin line. The second definition and foundation of all four principles is where you must set your intention.

Having regard for your own happiness is a perfectly succinct way, to sum up, the meaning of self-love as it pertains to 4Self. It's by no mistake that self-love is the first principle of 4Self. Loving yourself makes the other tenets attainable. Without it, they are impossible to truly achieve.

Sounds simple? I know it isn't, but you have to work on it at all costs to live the life you deserve. Start by being honest with yourself and think of what's holding you back from loving yourself fully. It could be a singular thing or multiple situations, but either way, the key is finding the root cause.

Dig deep and find your demons so you can fight and remove them from your life. Holding on to past guilt and not forgiving yourself will hinder your ability to love yourself completely. Also, thoughts of guilt that self-love is selfish, need to be released immediately. Remember, you can't correctly love anyone else until you love yourself.

At the beginning of my separation, I had no interest in my well-being; I just wanted my marriage repaired at any cost. I disregarded the dark feelings I often felt during the year before we separated and continued to be in denial about my marriage that had been broken long ago. Having little regard for my happiness caused me to hold onto something that had been gone for a long time.

However, on the flip side of self-love, as mentioned in Merriam's first definition, my conceit-driven ego couldn't accept what I viewed as a failure. Yeah, that line was really thin for me. I skipped right over it into egomania territory, determined on fixing the unfixable. I was fighting so hard to 'win' that I forgot what I was fighting for.

Truthfully, at this point it was no longer about being with the man I loved, but more about satisfying my constant need to triumph. What's worse, by now I had already fallen out of what I considered at the time to be love, and was merely on a conquest to prove a moot point. Thankfully, he didn't want me back, so it was eventually over.

My lack of self-love during this time also triggered the breakdown of my self-respect and self-esteem, and voided my self-care. But once I started working on loving myself again, remembering my worth and more significantly forgiving myself for the lack of regard I had for my own good, everything changed.

Immediately, my mindset shifted, and I knew that I was done with the charade of holding onto a dead marriage. Being honest with yourself and willing to work on the things that have caused both emotional and mental trauma are the precepts of loving yourself and believing that you're number one.

Self-Respect

I disrespected myself so many times during the separation—from begging him repeatedly to come back even after he made it clear that he was done, to the infamous overnight mishap in the Bronx. I felt less than worthy therefore allowing and accepting intolerable behavior to happen and it wasn't just during the separation.

When I found out about his 'emotional affair', I felt completely gutted and sick to my stomach. But after my enraged confrontation, I never really addressed the situation again out of fear; not fear of physical reprisal, but fear that he would bolt if I demanded anything from him or asked him to change.

I was so fearful of him leaving the marriage that after my initial anger about the affair, I was willing to ignore my hurt, avoid asking questions about the other woman, and continue as if nothing happened. I lost all self-respect and have no one to blame but myself, because I allowed it to happen.

Respecting yourself means knowing who you are and valuing your worth. It's understanding your limitations while standing firm in your beliefs, even at the sign of opposition. It's about being good to yourself and others while not being a doormat or an attention seeker.

A good way to start getting to know yourself is to fill out what I call 'a personal interview'. It's a list of questions, such as favorite color or podcast which, though simple in nature, helps to make you think about your likes and dislikes.

I came up with the idea at fourteen years old when I was in boarding school. I wanted to learn and document more about myself and my friends without relying on pictures. You can download a free copy of a

personal   interview   by   going   to
https://naudialorraine.com/ynonbpi

When you respect your worth and know that you're number one, you don't sit in a car all night waiting for someone who does not want you. #justsaying.

Self-respect is a crucial part of the 4Self system; it sets the foundation for self-esteem and helps to anchor personal development.

Self Esteem

Even after leaving my homeland at a young age and moving to another, then going to boarding school, then moving countries again, my self-esteem still remained entirely in check. I'm fortunate to have been raised by amazing parents who fostered my healthy self-esteem from a young age. In particular, when my dad would always remind me that I was number one or my mom eagerly fostering my creativity.

But even with my healthy self-esteem, I couldn't escape falling to bouts of self-loathing and a lack of confidence. From the onset of the separation, I took full blame; it was my fault entirely and I announced that to the few with whom I shared my devastation.

My despair and abhorrence only increased after the couples' therapy session when the allegedly neutral therapist announced that, just by listening to me, she could tell it was my fault, and requested to start separate sessions with me first.

What?! Utterly unheard of and beyond unprofessional but sadly, very true. As I mentioned earlier in the book, as we walked out of her office, Josh looked at me and said, "You see, even she thinks it's your fault." *Gag.*

I continued to blame only myself for the separation until the truth eventually dawned on me that both of us were at fault, not just me. Going to work every day to a job that I enjoyed at the time helped tremendously in rebuilding my low self-esteem.

But nothing helped more than my renewed faith in God despite the circumstances, and the love and support of my closest family and friends. They never gave up on me and were always there to give words of encouragement or lend a listening ear when I needed to vent, which was often!

When suffering from low self-esteem, it's important to surround yourself with positivity to help build your confidence. Having an encouraging support group of family, friends, or mentors is vital, as is removing negative people from your life.

Focusing on something other than the problem—whether it's work or a project—increases your self-worth, allowing you to feel more secure. Vulnerability heightens when you lack self-esteem which leads to making bad decisions. Feeling like you're not worthy of someone else's love is tragic and will always end badly.

That's why it's so important to build yourself back up after falling down. Regaining your self-esteem must be a priority for you in your everyday life as you work on your personal development.

As well as self-love and self-respect, self-esteem is a fundamental principle of 4Self, empowering you to feel deserving of much better. Because you *are* worth it.

Self-Care

When you're emotionally and mentally drained and feel down in the dumps, the last thing you want to think about is self-care. If you no longer love or respect yourself that much, taking care of you is not a concern.

But truthfully, self-care is the most straightforward principle of 4Self because it doesn't take much emotional or mental effort like the other three do. Some simple ways to self-care include taking a lovely walk, reading, having quiet time, or just taking a moment to focus on your breathing.

However, being the most natural principle to employ doesn't make it less vital. Self-care is a necessary and beneficial step in your wellness routine, and should be followed vigorously. During my journey, I found that focusing on health and travel were the perfect forms of self-care that I needed.

I started exercising again, eating right, and glowing from the inside out, enjoying every moment of a healthier me. But traveling is what really changed my life and corrected my mindset. Particularly, when I embarked upon my life-changing trip to Belgium, which became the crowning moment of my personal development journey.

Traveling solo is so good for your soul, as it allows you to open up to more experiences and people, because you have no one holding you back. It also gives you ample time to be in thought without any distractions, which is essential for healing a broken heart.

I had the best time taking the chocolate course, visiting smaller villages outside Brussels, and meeting lovely people—all the while feeling like I could actually breathe for the first time since the separation. Before the trip, I was already working on myself using the other three principles of 4Self, so this became the fulfillment of my rebirth. I laughed out loud without a care in the world and enjoyed every single moment; my life felt recharged and revived.

Once and for all, I was free. I accepted that my marriage had failed and felt so much gratitude for the lessons learned along the way. I no longer needed to be with him to keep up appearances. I was totally over it and happier than ever.

I will always treasure the peace that I felt on my last night in Brussels. My life was back in order, and it felt incredible. Simply put, self-care is about taking care of yourself and being good to your mind, body, and soul.

Now that you know what 4Self is all about, be inspired to use the system as you work on your personal development goals and well-being. Taking only fifteen minutes every day to work on each principle will help you tremendously on your journey, but you have to be dedicated.

Commit to following the guidelines, especially using your journal. Being able to go back and track your progress does wonders for your development. You only have one life, and you deserve to live it to the max. Don't allow negative thoughts to continue to prevent you from wanting and doing more.

Personal development is an ongoing process that must be taken seriously. With the help of 4Self, start focusing on your growth and accomplishing your goals in earnest.

Acknowledgments

Wow, there were some really tough moments writing this book, reliving embarrassing situations and times where I totally lacked self-awareness. However, I was committed to sharing my story to prevent at least one person from repeating my mistakes.

Through it all, I've had the amazing love and support from some pretty awesome people with my parents being at the top of the list. Mom & dad, I love you both to bits and could never live long enough to thank you for all that you've done for me and to show how much I love and appreciate you.

To my other half, the true love of my life, thank you for always being my rock, for not taking my crap and putting me in my place when necessary, lol. To Faith, Lyndon, Christine, Maddi, Lexi I love you all so much. To my extended family & friends-much love.

To Lise, my fab writing coach, thank you for your continued support. To Marie, my writing accountability partner and friend thank you for always listening and cheers to our Saturday morning calls! To the awesome SPS community- I appreciate you.

Final words from the author

Thanks so much for reading- you're awesome! I hope that you were inspired by my not so conventional journey to be the best you, love yourself unconditionally and believe that you're number one!

I'm on a mission to spread my mantra, 'You're number one, now believe it!' around the world. With the belief that personal development is the cornerstone of all personal & business relationships and without it failure is inevitable.

If you know someone who this book may help, please feel free to share with them. Also, if you enjoyed it I would love if you could leave a review on Amazon.com. No pressure!

Now that you know a little about me, feel free to reach out and connect at naudia@naudialorraine or one of my social media channels below and don't forget to download your Personal Interview by going to: *www.naudialorraine.com/YNONBPI.*

Instagram: @naudialorraine
Facebook: @naudialorraine
shop.naudialorraine.com

With gratitude,

Xo, Naudia Lorraine

Made in the
USA
Middletown, DE